The Geography of Woman
A Journey Through the Ages of Life

By : Ed Merid

© Copyright 2024 Ed Merid - All Rights Reserved.

Copyright and Disclaimer

The contents of this book may not be reproduced, duplicated, or transmitted without the written permission of the author. Under no circumstances shall the publisher, or the author, be held legally liable for any monetary or non-monetary damages or losses resulting from the information contained in this book, whether directly or indirectly.

Legal Notice:

This book is copyrighted and is intended for personal use only. You may not modify, distribute, sell, use, quote, or paraphrase any part or content of this book without the consent of the author or publisher.

Table of Contents

Introduction

Every woman carries within her a unique landscape, shaped by time, experiences, and emotions. Like a traveler discovering unknown lands, she crosses territories she did not suspect at the beginning of her journey. Innocent childhood, tumultuous adolescence, adventurous youth, and thoughtful maturity: so many landscapes, each marked by its reliefs, its storms, and its clearings.

But the geography of women is not limited to fixed landmarks. It is fluid, evolving, shaped by external events, but also by internal revolutions. At each age, new horizons emerge, peaks to climb, rivers to cross, and deserts to tame.

This book is a map, a compass to understand the different ages of a woman's life, by exploring the pivotal moments that shape her and the transformations that transform her. Through the stories and reflections, you will discover that each step is not an end, but a new step in the infinite richness of the feminine journey.

Perhaps you will recognize yourself in these pages, or perhaps you will find echoes of lives that you have not yet explored. No matter the age or the moment of the journey, this book is intended to be a companion for those who wish to understand the complex and multidimensional beauty of women, seen as a rich and constantly evolving territory.

Welcome to this journey through the ages, where each year is a new land, each emotion a path, and each experience a treasure to discover.

Chapter 1: Childhood - The Innocent Plain

The odyssey of women finds its humble beginnings in the vast, unblemished canvas of childhood. This pristine expanse, untrammeled by the complexities that lie ahead, exists as a realm of pure potential, a blank slate upon which the first brushstrokes of identity and self-discovery are tentatively etched.

Within this tranquil domain, a young girl's world revolves around the simple pleasures of play, imagination, and the budding bonds that gently mold her incipient sense of self. Curiosity reigns supreme, as every new sight, sound, and sensation is met with an insatiable thirst for exploration, a desire to unravel the mysteries that surround her. It is a time of uncomplicated joys, where the boundaries between reality and fantasy are delightfully blurred, and the constraints of adulthood have yet to encroach upon the vibrant tapestry of childhood.

Yet, even in this realm of seeming stasis, the gentle currents of growth and change flow ever-present, if imperceptible at first glance. Subtle shifts in perspectives, emotions, and relationships begin to sculpt the nascent contours of a child's burgeoning identity. The unblemished canvas may appear unchanging on the surface, but upon closer inspection, one can discern the delicate processes that lay the groundwork for the remarkable metamorphoses that will inevitably follow.

As the journey through the ages commences, this pristine expanse serves as the point of embarkation, a sanctuary where the seeds of selfhood are sown and the first exploratory tendrils of self-discovery take root. It is a realm of pure potentiality, where the boundless possibilities of life stretch out like an endless horizon, awaiting the eventual blossoming of growth and maturation.

1.1: Self-Discovery

Childhood is often perceived as a period of simplicity and innocence, a time when a girl's life is filled with play, exploration, and imagination. However, beneath this surface of carefree joy lies a powerful and essential process: the discovery of self. It is during these early years that a girl begins to form a sense of who she is, through experiences, relationships, and a growing understanding of the world around her.

This process of self-discovery can be compared to a blank canvas on which the first strokes of identity are painted. At first, the strokes may seem faint, tentative, but as each day passes, the canvas fills with vibrant colors and patterns, each one representing a new layer of her evolving self. These brushstrokes are shaped by interactions with family, friends, and the environment, all of which help her to define her sense of being.

From a very young age, a child begins to recognize that she is separate from others. This recognition often starts with something as simple as looking in a mirror and realizing, "That's me." This awareness, known as self-recognition, is a pivotal moment in the journey toward understanding identity. It is the first step toward realizing that she has her own thoughts, feelings, and desires that are distinct from those of the people around her. In some cultures, this realization is seen as an important milestone. The ancient Greeks, for example, emphasized the importance of knowing oneself, a concept they called "gnothi seauton", meaning "know thyself."

As she begins to explore the world, a young girl's sense of self expands and evolves. Simple, everyday experiences play a crucial role in this development. Consider the excitement of learning to ride a bike. At first, the task seems daunting, balancing on two wheels feels impossible. But with persistence and support from those around her, she eventually gains the confidence to ride independently. This triumph becomes more than just a physical accomplishment; it becomes a building block in her growing identity. She learns that she is capable of achieving difficult things through effort and perseverance.

Similarly, social interactions in childhood offer essential lessons about self-discovery. Whether playing with other children at school or negotiating the rules of a game, she learns about trust, friendship, and boundaries. These interactions help her understand her place within a group, and she begins to form a social identity. For example, when she makes a new friend at school, she starts to see herself as part of a relationship, learning that she can be valued for who she is. Conversely, moments of conflict or rejection, such as not being chosen for a game, teach her resilience and the ability to bounce back from disappointment.

Books and stories also play a significant role in shaping a young girl's sense of self. When she reads about characters like Jo March from "Little Women", she sees herself reflected in their journeys of self-discovery, their triumphs, and their struggles. Jo's determination to carve out her own path, despite societal expectations, can inspire young readers to think about their own aspirations and dreams. Through these stories, a child learns that her identity is not something fixed or predetermined, but something she can shape and grow over time.

In many ways, the journey of self-discovery is like walking through a vast and colorful garden. Each new experience is like a flower blooming along the path, adding beauty and complexity to her sense of self. Some flowers, like the joy of making a new friend, bloom brightly and easily. Others, like the lessons learned from failure or loss, may be more difficult to nurture but are no less essential to the richness of her identity.

While much of self-discovery happens through personal experiences, it is also a collaborative process. The people in a young girl's life, her parents, siblings, teachers, and friends, play a crucial role in helping her navigate this journey. Parents provide guidance and encouragement, offering her a safe space to explore who she is. Teachers and mentors help her discover her interests and talents, whether it's through academics, sports, or the arts. Friends and peers offer opportunities for social learning, teaching her about cooperation, empathy, and belonging.

Take the example of Helen Keller, whose early experiences with her teacher, Anne Sullivan, illustrate how crucial guidance can be in the process of self-discovery. Keller's ability to learn language despite being deaf and blind opened up a world of understanding and self-awareness for her. This journey of discovery helped Keller develop into an influential advocate for disability rights, showing how powerful and transformative the process of self-discovery can be when nurtured by supportive relationships.

However, self-discovery is not always a smooth or straightforward journey. There are moments of doubt, uncertainty, and confusion. A young girl might struggle with questions about who she is, what she believes, or what she wants to become. These questions, while difficult, are an important part of the process. They encourage her to reflect deeply on her experiences and values, ultimately leading to a more authentic and grounded sense of self.

It's significant for parents, teachers, and mentors to create an environment where children feel safe to explore and express themselves. Encouraging curiosity, celebrating achievements, and offering support in times of difficulty all contribute to a child's confidence in her own identity. Simple activities, like asking a child to share what made them happy or sad during the day, can foster emotional awareness and self-reflection. Similarly, acknowledging their strengths and encouraging them to pursue what they love can help children feel proud of who they are becoming.

In conclusion, self-discovery in childhood is an ongoing and dynamic process. It is shaped by both internal reflections and external experiences. Every triumph and challenge, every friendship and conflict, contributes to the ever-evolving portrait of whom a young girl is. Just like an artist carefully adding layers to a painting, a child gradually builds her identity, one experience at a time, creating a vibrant and unique picture of herself that will continue to evolve throughout her life.

Practical Takeaways:
- Encourage Reflection: Take time to ask children what they learned or felt during the day. Encouraging them to articulate their thoughts helps build emotional and self-awareness.
- Celebrate Achievements: No matter how small, acknowledging successes builds confidence and a sense of capability, laying the foundation for a strong identity.
- Foster Curiosity: Provide opportunities for children to explore new hobbies, interests, and skills. Encourage their curiosity, as this helps them discover their passions and strengths.

1.2: The Construction of Identity

As a girl moves through the landscape of childhood, her identity begins to take shape, constructed piece by piece through her interactions with the world around her. While the journey of self-discovery starts with the recognition of being separate and distinct, the construction of identity involves layering experiences, relationships, and cultural influences that define her growing sense of self. Identity is not formed in isolation; it is influenced and molded by the people and environments that surround her, becoming a multifaceted, evolving creation.

The foundation of a child's identity is laid from her earliest moments. The warm embrace of her parents, the soothing voice of a caregiver, and the secure environment of her home all contribute to her earliest sense of belonging and safety. These early experiences teach her that she is cared for and valued. According to psychologist

John Bowlby's attachment theory, these emotional bonds are crucial in shaping how a child views herself and how she will relate to others later in life. If her early environment is nurturing and consistent, she learns that the world is a safe place and that she is worthy of love. If her environment is chaotic or neglectful, this can impact her sense of security and self-worth.

As she grows, the child begins to explore the world outside of her immediate family. Her first interactions with peers, whether at school or on the playground, introduce new dynamics into the construction of her identity. At this stage, she learns about social roles, cooperation, and individuality. Playing with others teaches her how to assert herself, negotiate, and navigate conflict. If she is part of a group of friends, she starts to see herself in relation to others, understanding her role within the group. For instance, she might identify as the leader, the peacemaker, or the creative one. These early social roles begin to shape her self-image.

Books, media, and stories also play a significant role in this process. A child who reads about characters like Matilda, a young girl who uses her intelligence and resilience to overcome challenges, may begin to see herself as capable and strong. The stories she consumes become mirrors, reflecting back ideas about whom she can be and what is possible in her life. Just as Jo March from "Little Women" inspires young readers to think beyond societal expectations, the characters in a child's favorite books offer a framework for imagining their own potential.

However, identity construction is not a linear or easy process. Just as a house requires a strong foundation and careful attention to detail, the building of identity involves trial and error, as well as external influences. A child might try on different identities, much like trying on clothes, to see what fits. One day, she might aspire to be an artist, and the next, a scientist. This experimentation is an essential part of growth, helping her refine her sense of self. Encouraging this exploration without judgment allows a child the freedom to develop in her own unique way.

The construction of identity is also influenced by culture and societal expectations. For example, a girl growing up in a family that values academic achievement may begin to see herself as a scholar, with her self-worth tied to her performance in school. Cultural norms about gender, race, and class also shape identity, often subconsciously. A girl who sees powerful role models in her community or in the media may feel more confident in her own potential, whereas a girl who feels her identity is underrepresented or marginalized may struggle with feelings of inadequacy.

Take the case of artist Frida Kahlo. From a young age, Kahlo's identity was shaped by her Mexican heritage, her experience with physical disability, and her exposure to art. The pain she experienced, both physical and emotional, became central to her artistic expression, and her identity as an artist was deeply intertwined with her sense of self. Her childhood experiences were like the early bricks in the construction of her identity, each layer added depth and complexity to the person she would become.

As a child continues to build her identity, the support of family and mentors becomes crucial. Parents and caregivers act as guides, helping her navigate the sometimes-confusing terrain of growing up. Positive reinforcement, constructive feedback, and a safe space to express herself help her develop a strong, resilient identity. The role of educators and mentors is equally important. A teacher who recognizes a child's unique strengths can help her see herself in a new light, fostering a sense of competence and self-efficacy.

Identity construction is also closely tied to the challenges a child faces. Adversity, whether in the form of bullying, academic struggles, or family difficulties, forces her to develop coping strategies that become integral to her sense of self. For instance, a child who experiences rejection or failure might initially struggle with feelings of inadequacy. However, with the right support, she can learn to view challenges as opportunities for growth. This process of overcoming obstacles adds resilience to her identity, teaching her that she is capable of bouncing back from hardship.

Historical figures like Maya Angelou provide powerful examples of how early experiences shape identity. Angelou's childhood was marked by trauma, but through her experiences and the support of mentors, she emerged as a powerful voice in literature and civil rights. Her identity as a writer and activist was shaped not only by her personal hardships but also by the love and guidance she received from those who encouraged her to use her voice.

The construction of identity is an ongoing process, one that continues into adulthood. Yet the foundations laid in childhood are crucial. The experiences, relationships, and challenges a child encounters during this time provide the building blocks for the person she will become. Each interaction, whether positive or negative, adds a layer to her identity, helping her to understand who she is and where she fits in the world.

Practical Takeaways:
- Provide a Safe Environment: Ensure that children feel loved and valued. A secure foundation at home allows them to explore their identity with confidence.
- Encourage Exploration: Let children try different activities, hobbies, and roles without pressure. Exploration is key to discovering their strengths and interests.
- Support Through Challenges: Teach children that adversity is a natural part of life. Help them see challenges as opportunities for growth, which strengthens their resilience.
- Set an Example: Kids pick up skills from watching you. Show them what it means to embrace their identity by modeling confidence, kindness, and authenticity in your own life.

Chapter 2: Adolescence - The Volcanoes of Transformation

The serene meadows of childhood eventually give way to a landscape of profound transformation, the volcanic terrain of adolescence. This tumultuous expanse, marked by seismic upheavals and eruptions of change, represents a pivotal juncture in the journey of women. A crucible in which the once-tranquil waters of youth are disrupted by the molten flows of physical, emotional, and psychological metamorphosis.

Akin to the earth's restless tectonic plates, the forces of puberty converge, triggering a series of cataclysmic shifts that reverberate through every aspect of a young woman's being. Hormonal surges, akin to subterranean magma, catalyze the remarkable physical transformations that signal the transition from girl to woman. Meanwhile, the once-familiar landscapes of childhood give way to unfamiliar, ever-shifting emotional terrains, riddled with the fissures of insecurity, self-doubt, and the burning desire for independence.

Within this volatile expanse, the once-sturdy foundations of identity are subjected to intense pressures, as the eruptions of self-discovery and self-expression intermingle with the seismic rumblings of peer influence and societal expectations. The quest for belonging and self-actualization becomes a perilous trek across fields of emotional lava, where every step is fraught with the potential for scorching missteps or transcendent awakenings.

Yet, amidst the chaos and turmoil, there exists a remarkable opportunity for growth and resilience. Just as the most awe-inspiring landscapes are forged by the relentless forces of nature, so too does the crucible of adolescence mold the strength, adaptability, and self-awareness that will become indispensable assets in the chapters that lie ahead.

By navigating the treacherous terrain of this transformative phase, a young woman emerges from the proverbial ashes, tempered by the fires of experience. She is imbued with a deeper understanding of her own power, her own potential, and her own unique place within the ever-evolving geography of women.

2.1: The Eruption of Emotions

Adolescence is often referred to as a turbulent time, marked by intense emotional shifts that can feel as unpredictable and powerful as a volcanic eruption. During this stage, a young woman undergoes significant physical, emotional, and psychological changes, all fueled by the surging hormones that accompany puberty. These hormonal shifts are much like the molten magma beneath the earth's surface, at times calm, but when stirred, they erupt, altering the landscape of her emotional world.

At the heart of this emotional upheaval is the complex interplay of identity formation, peer relationships, and the growing desire for independence. A young girl, who once found comfort and stability in childhood's routines, now faces new challenges that stir feelings of insecurity, confusion, and sometimes even rebellion. These feelings are normal, yet they can be overwhelming for someone navigating the transition from childhood to adulthood. Just as volcanoes create both destruction and new landforms, the emotional eruptions of adolescence pave the way for new emotional depths, maturity, and self-awareness.

Physical and Hormonal Changes:

The onset of puberty marks the beginning of this emotional rollercoaster. Hormonal changes, such as increased levels of estrogen and progesterone, contribute to mood swings, heightened sensitivity, and new feelings that a young girl may struggle to understand. These surges can cause her to react more intensely to situations that she once found manageable. One moment, she might feel exhilarated by the prospect of a new friendship or crush; the next, she could be overwhelmed by feelings of sadness or frustration.

For example, the first experience of menstruation, a key milestone in female puberty, often brings not only physical discomfort but also emotional vulnerability. For many girls, the changes in their bodies are accompanied by feelings of embarrassment or anxiety. They may worry about how their changing bodies will be perceived by others, especially their peers. This can lead to self-consciousness and a heightened sense of emotional fragility.

Social Dynamics and Peer Pressure:

In addition to hormonal changes, social dynamics during adolescence play a significant role in the emotional landscape. Friendships become more complex, and the pressure to fit in with peer groups can create intense emotional conflict. Adolescents are particularly sensitive to acceptance and rejection from their peers, and even minor social slights can feel catastrophic.

Imagine a scenario where a young girl is excluded from a social gathering or teased by classmates. The feelings of isolation or embarrassment that arise in these moments can be deeply painful, triggering an emotional reaction far stronger than the situation may seem to warrant. This heightened sensitivity is normal but difficult to navigate, and it can leave her feeling as though she's constantly balancing on the edge of an emotional cliff.

For many adolescents, peer pressure becomes a major source of emotional stress. The desire to be liked and accepted by a group can lead to internal conflict, particularly when the values of the group clash with her personal beliefs. Whether it's pressure to conform to certain beauty standards, engage in risky behavior, or suppress her true self to avoid judgment, these external forces can contribute to emotional turmoil. The young woman may feel torn between staying true to herself and conforming to fit in, a struggle that can lead to frustration, anxiety, and even feelings of inadequacy.

The Desire for Independence:

At the same time, the growing desire for independence adds another layer to the emotional complexity of adolescence. A young woman begins to seek autonomy, pushing back against the authority of parents and other adults. This newfound desire for freedom often manifests as defiance or rebellion, as she tests the boundaries of her relationships and asserts her individuality.

This search for independence is essential to her development, but it also brings emotional challenges. Conflicts with parents, who may still see her as a child, can create feelings of frustration and resentment. She may feel misunderstood, as though the people who once provided comfort and security now stand in the way of her personal growth. This can lead to moments of intense emotional outburst, where her anger or sadness feels all-consuming.

A young woman's struggle for independence is also linked to her developing sense of identity. As she starts to make decisions about her interests, friendships, and future aspirations, she faces emotional challenges that test her resolve and self-confidence. The fear of making the wrong choices or disappointing those around her can cause anxiety, while the excitement of newfound freedom can bring feelings of empowerment.

Navigating Emotional Eruptions:

Navigating the emotional eruptions of adolescence requires both self-awareness and support from those around her. It's important for parents, teachers, and mentors to understand that these emotional fluctuations are not only normal but necessary for growth. By providing a safe and supportive space for her to express her feelings, adults can help her develop emotional intelligence and resilience.

Open communication is key. Encouraging a young woman to talk about her feelings can help her make sense of her emotional responses and learn how to manage them. Rather than dismissing her emotions as "just a phase," adults should validate her feelings, helping her understand that it's okay to experience intense emotions and that these moments are part of the larger process of growing up.

At the same time, teaching her strategies for managing these emotional highs and lows can make a significant difference. Techniques such as journaling, mindfulness exercises, and deep breathing can help her regulate her emotions and prevent her from feeling overwhelmed. These tools offer a way for her to process what she's feeling without being consumed by the intensity of her emotions.

The Long-Term Impact of Emotional Growth:

While the emotional turbulence of adolescence may feel overwhelming, it is an essential part of a young woman's development. These emotional experiences, though challenging, lay the groundwork for emotional maturity and self-awareness. Just as the molten lava of a volcano eventually cools to form new landscapes, the emotional surges of adolescence help shape a woman's emotional resilience and depth.

By learning to navigate these emotional eruptions, a young woman becomes better equipped to handle the complexities of adult relationships, career challenges, and personal growth. The ability to understand and regulate her emotions becomes one of her greatest strengths, allowing her to build meaningful connections with others and maintain a strong sense of self, even in the face of adversity.

Practical Takeaways:

- Validate Emotions: Acknowledge that intense emotions are part of adolescence. Let young women know it's okay to feel deeply, and encourage them to talk about their feelings.
- Teach Coping Strategies: Introduce tools like mindfulness, journaling, and breathing exercises to help manage overwhelming emotions.

- Support Independence: Understand that the desire for autonomy is normal. Encourage independent decision-making, while offering guidance and support when needed.

2.2: The Quest for Belonging

Adolescence is a time when the need for belonging takes on new meaning and urgency. As a young woman navigates the emotional peaks and valleys of this transformative stage, the desire to be accepted by her peers becomes one of her most pressing motivations. No longer content to simply belong to her family, she seeks validation and acceptance from friends, classmates, and social circles. This quest for belonging is not only an emotional journey but also a formative experience that teaches her about relationships, self-worth, and the importance of authenticity.

During this period, social acceptance can feel like a matter of survival. Adolescents are incredibly attuned to their peers' opinions, and fitting in becomes a priority as she works to establish her identity outside the family unit. The desire for belonging, while universal, can lead her to adopt behaviors, values, and even identities that may not truly align with who she is. For a young woman, this quest is both a journey of self-discovery and, at times, a path fraught with challenges.

The Role of Peer Influence:

As young women transition into adolescence, their social worlds expand significantly. The influence of friends and peers often becomes stronger than that of family members, and peer approval is sought as a way of affirming identity. Adolescents are especially susceptible to peer pressure, which can shape everything from fashion choices and music preferences to beliefs and behavior.

Peer groups can offer a sense of solidarity and companionship, providing a safe space where a young woman feels understood and valued. Belonging to a group can be empowering, as it assures her that she's not alone in her struggles or her experiences. However, peer groups also present challenges, especially if a young woman feels pressured to compromise her values or ignore her individuality in order to fit in.

Consider a young girl who joins a social circle that places a high value on certain brands of clothing or physical appearance. She may feel compelled to conform to these expectations, even if it doesn't align with her personal preferences or family values. While this adaptation is part of the normal quest for belonging, it can also create internal conflict, as she wrestles with the need to fit in and the desire to stay true to herself. Balancing these two desires is a central theme of adolescence and a skill that will serve her throughout life.

The Search for Authenticity:

The adolescent quest for belonging is complicated by the equally strong desire for authenticity. While a young woman wants to fit in, she also yearns to be accepted for whom she truly is. This internal struggle, between conforming to social expectations and expressing her authentic self, can be both empowering and frustrating. Adolescents are often acutely aware when they are putting on a facade, and the conflict between self-expression and social acceptance can cause significant emotional tension.

This tension between authenticity and acceptance is particularly challenging in today's digital age, where social media amplifies the need for approval. Adolescents typically present curated versions of themselves online, aiming to gain likes, followers, or positive comments. This creates a delicate balance between self-presentation and genuine self-expression. For many, the pressure to maintain a certain image online intensifies the quest for belonging, while making it harder to connect with their true selves. Social media can be a powerful tool for connection, but it can also leave young women feeling isolated or inauthentic if they are constantly comparing themselves to idealized images or altering their behavior to meet online expectations.

Navigating Friendships and Group Dynamics:

During adolescence, friendships take on a new depth and significance. Friends become confidants, allies, and sources of support, helping a young woman navigate the ups and downs of her teenage years. These relationships offer her a sense of belonging outside her family, giving her a space where she feels understood and valued. However, friendships during adolescence can be complex, as they are often characterized by shifting alliances, jealousy, and competition.

Learning to navigate group dynamics and handle conflicts is a valuable part of the adolescent experience. A young woman may experience the pain of being excluded from a social event or the joy of finding a friend who truly understands her. Each of these experiences contributes to her understanding of relationships and teaches her about the qualities she values in friends. Moments of exclusion or betrayal, while painful, also offer valuable lessons in resilience and self-worth. They remind her that true belonging is not about changing herself to fit in, but about finding people who appreciate her for who she is.

An important aspect of friendships during adolescence is the opportunity they provide for young women to practice empathy and learn about others' experiences. Friendships expose her to different perspectives, helping her develop a more nuanced understanding of the world. A friend from a different cultural or socioeconomic background, for instance, can broaden her perspective and help her appreciate the diversity of human experience. These relationships also teach her about loyalty, compassion, and forgiveness, qualities that will be invaluable throughout her life.

Building Self-Worth Through Belonging:

The adolescent quest for belonging is not just about finding external validation; it is also an essential part of building self-worth. Through her interactions with peers, a young woman learns about her own strengths, values, and boundaries. While positive friendships can boost her confidence and reinforce her self-worth, negative experiences, such as bullying or exclusion, can be deeply damaging.

Encouraging young women to value themselves independently of social approval is essential for their development. Activities that foster self-discovery, such as sports, arts, or volunteering, can help build confidence and provide a sense of purpose that is not tied to peer approval. When a young woman understands her intrinsic worth, she is less likely to compromise her values or seek validation through unhealthy relationships. By building a foundation of self-worth, she can approach friendships with a healthy sense of independence, finding a balance between her need for connection and her desire for authenticity.

The Long-Term Impact of Belonging:

The lessons learned from the quest for belonging extend far beyond adolescence. The ability to form meaningful relationships, balance authenticity with social acceptance, and maintain self-worth are skills that serve a woman throughout her life. While the adolescent years may be marked by uncertainty and the intense need for peer approval, these experiences ultimately help her develop a more secure sense of self.

By learning to navigate the complexities of friendships and group dynamics, a young woman gains resilience and a deeper understanding of what true belonging means. She realizes that real connection is not about fitting into a mold, but about being valued for her unique qualities. This insight, gained through the challenges and triumphs of adolescence, becomes a guiding principle as she enters adulthood, helping her to build relationships based on mutual respect, understanding, and genuine acceptance.

Practical Takeaways:

1. Encourage Authenticity: Support young women in expressing their true selves, even if it means standing out. Remind them that they deserve to be valued for who they are, not who they pretend to be.

2. Promote Healthy Friendships: Encourage young women to seek friendships that are supportive and positive. Help them recognize the difference between healthy friendships and relationships that require them to compromise their values.

3. Limit Social Media Pressure: Discuss the impact of social media and encourage a balanced approach. Remind them that online personas don't always reflect reality and that their worth is not defined by likes or followers.

4. Build Self-Worth: Encourage activities that foster self-confidence and a sense of purpose. Whether through sports, arts, or community involvement, these activities help develop a strong sense of self-worth that is independent of peer approval.

Chapter 3: Young Adulthood - The Desert of Independence

As the tumultuous landscapes of adolescence gradually recede, the journey of women ushers forth a vast, arid expanse, the desert of independence. This sun-baked terrain, at once harsh and liberating, represents a pivotal phase in the unfolding saga of self-discovery and self-actualization. The fires of youthful ambition and the thirst for autonomy are tested against the unforgiving elements of adulthood.

Within this parched domain, the young woman embarks on a quest to forge her own oasis, a sanctuary where she can cultivate the seeds of her aspirations and nurture the blossoming of her unique identity. Freed from the constraints of childhood and the tempestuous upheavals of adolescence, she finds herself navigating uncharted territories, where every step is a testament to her burgeoning independence and her unwavering determination to carve out her place in the world.

Yet, this newfound liberation is not without its challenges. The desert of independence is a harsh mistress, presenting a gauntlet of obstacles and trials that demand resilience, adaptability, and an unwavering commitment to personal growth. From the scorching sun of financial pressures to the shifting sands of career uncertainties, every aspect of this arid expanse tests the mettle of the young woman's spirit.

It is within this crucible that the true essence of womanhood is tempered. The journey across the desert of independence demands a delicate balance between self-reliance and a willingness to seek guidance, between the pursuit of personal dreams and the recognition of one's role within the broader tapestry of society. Each step, each mirage overcome, and each oasis discovered adds another layer of depth and wisdom to the ever-evolving tapestry of identity.

As the young woman emerges from this transformative phase, she carries with her the hard-won lessons of self-sufficiency, resilience, and the deep realization that real independence is a lifelong process of self-actualization and self-discovery rather than just a destination. With each grain of sand that slips through her fingers, she learns to embrace the beauty and power of her own autonomy, forever intertwined with the ever-evolving landscapes of womanhood.

3.1: Finding Your Way

Stepping into young adulthood is like entering a vast and unfamiliar desert, where the sense of direction is often unclear, and the path forward can feel overwhelming. As a young woman moves through this stage, she is confronted with choices that will shape her future, choices related to career, relationships, and personal values. While this period brings newfound freedom and opportunities, it also introduces uncertainty, fear, and the pressure to succeed.

In many ways, young adulthood is defined by the search for direction. As childhood and adolescence recede into the past, a young woman must navigate this new landscape largely on her own. Gone are the structured environments of school and home, replaced by the uncharted territory of independence. While exciting, this transition also brings challenges that can leave her feeling lost and unsure of her next steps.

The Desire for Purpose:

At the heart of this period is a deep desire for purpose. A young woman in her early twenties is often grappling with questions about her career and personal goals. She may have completed her education or embarked on a new job, but she's likely still searching for a sense of meaning in what she does. This search for purpose is frequently accompanied by pressure, both external and internal, to find the "right" path, a decision that can feel overwhelming.

Take, for example, the story of a young woman who is passionate about art but has chosen a more conventional career in finance because it seems more stable. She may feel torn between the security of a well-paying job and the pull of her creative passion. This kind of internal conflict is common during young adulthood, as women face the challenge of balancing practicality with their dreams.

In many cases, the societal expectations of success, often defined by financial independence, career advancement, and personal milestones, can cloud a young woman's understanding of what she truly wants. It's easy to get caught up in pursuing goals that don't align with her values, simply because they seem to be the markers of "success" that society holds up.

Exploring Identity and Values:

At the same time, this stage of life is a critical period for exploring identity. A young woman is not just figuring out what she wants to do, but also who she wants to be. The experiences of early adulthood challenge her to reflect on her core values and beliefs, as well as the type of person she aspires to become. It's a time when she begins to forge an identity that is separate from her family and peers, relying on her own sense of self to guide her decisions.

For many, this exploration of identity is tied to the people she meets and the environments she inhabits. The friendships, romantic relationships, and professional networks she builds during this time contribute significantly to her evolving sense of self. A woman may find that her values shift as she engages with new ideas and perspectives, or she may feel the need to assert her beliefs more strongly in the face of contrasting views.

Managing these social dynamics may be thrilling and difficult at the same time. There's often a desire to fit in with new peer groups, especially in professional settings, where networking and building relationships are key to success. However, the pressure to conform to the expectations of others can lead to a feeling of disconnection from one's true self. A young woman might find herself participating in activities or taking on roles that don't align with her core values, all in the effort to belong.

Embracing Uncertainty:

One of the most difficult aspects of this stage is learning to embrace uncertainty. In a culture that regularly promotes the idea of having a clear plan or path, it can be unsettling to realize that many of the answers won't come easily. A young woman may feel immense pressure to know exactly where she's going, but the reality is that young adulthood is more about the process of figuring things out than having all the answers.

Many women experience periods of doubt and indecision during this time. The question, "Am I doing the right thing?" frequently looms large, whether it has to do with a decision in life, a relationship, or a profession. This uncertainty can lead to anxiety, as it feels like every choice carries significant weight. However, it's important to recognize that uncertainty is a natural part of growth. Making mistakes, taking detours, and reevaluating one's goals are all essential to finding a path that is both meaningful and fulfilling.

It can be helpful for young women to give themselves permission to explore different options without feeling like every decision is final. Experimenting with new jobs, hobbies, or relationships can provide valuable insights into what feels right and what doesn't. Just like a traveler in a vast desert, the path forward may not always be straight or clear, but each step offers an opportunity to learn and grow.

The Importance of Mentorship and Support:

During this period of uncertainty, mentorship, and support networks become invaluable. A mentor, whether a family member, a professor, or a colleague, can offer guidance and perspective, helping a young woman navigate the difficult decisions she faces. Mentors can share their own experiences, providing reassurance that uncertainty is normal and that there is no one "right" way to build a life.

In addition to mentors, having a strong support network of friends and loved ones can make a significant difference. Surrounding oneself with people who offer encouragement, listen without judgment, and provide constructive advice can alleviate the feeling of isolation that often accompanies young adulthood. These relationships serve as emotional anchors, helping a young woman feel grounded even when the future seems uncertain.

Practical Strategies for Navigating Young Adulthood:

1. Your Values: Take time to reflect on what matters most to you. Write down your core values and revisit them when making important decisions. This will help ensure that your choices align with who you are and what you stand for.
2. Experiment with Different Paths: Don't be afraid to try new things. Whether it's taking a class in a subject you've never studied, starting a side project, or traveling, experimenting with different paths can help you discover what truly excites and fulfills you.
3. Find Mentors and Allies: Seek out people who inspire you and whose values align with yours. Their guidance and advice can provide clarity when you feel uncertain.
4. Embrace Mistakes: Understand that not every decision will lead to success, and that's okay. Mistakes are part of the learning process, and they often provide valuable insights that will guide you forward.
5. Create a Flexible Plan: While having goals is important, it's equally important to remain flexible. Life rarely follows a perfect script, and being open to change will help you adapt and thrive.

3.2: Learning Responsibilities

As a young woman steps further into the vast desert of independence, the weight of responsibility begins to settle on her shoulders. It is in this phase that she learns the true meaning of accountability, both to herself and to those around her. The freedom that comes with young adulthood is exciting, but it also demands a new level of maturity, self-discipline, and the ability to juggle multiple roles. For many, this period is marked by a series of firsts: first job, first apartment, first time managing finances independently. Each of these milestones brings with it a new set of responsibilities that must be learned and mastered.

The transition from adolescence to young adulthood is much like setting out on a journey across an arid desert. The path ahead can seem overwhelming, with no clear end in sight. However, each step forward, each challenge faced, helps to build resilience and confidence. Responsibilities that once felt daunting gradually become second nature, and the young woman begins to see herself as capable of handling the complexities of adult life.

Financial Independence and Management:

One of the most significant responsibilities that comes with young adulthood is financial independence. For many women, this is the first time they are solely responsible for managing their income, budgeting, and ensuring that they meet their financial obligations. Whether it's paying rent, managing student loan debt, or saving for future goals, financial management can feel overwhelming at first.

Learning how to create and stick to a budget is a key skill during this time. Without the safety net of parental support, a young woman must develop a sense of financial discipline, ensuring that her income covers her expenses while also saving for emergencies and future plans. Budgeting tools and apps can be incredibly helpful, providing a clear picture of where her money is going and helping her avoid the trap of living paycheck to paycheck.

This new financial responsibility is not just about paying bills; it's also about making decisions that align with her values and long-term goals. A young woman must decide how to allocate her resources, whether that means saving for further education, investing in her career, or simply enjoying her newfound independence. These decisions help to shape her future and give her a sense of control over her life.

However, financial independence also comes with challenges. It's easy to fall into the trap of overspending, particularly when faced with the pressures of keeping up with peers or indulging in the freedom that comes with having one's own income. Learning to balance the desire for short-term gratification with long-term financial stability is a critical lesson during this phase of life.

Balancing Work and Personal Life:

As a young woman navigates her career, she is also learning the delicate art of balancing work and personal life. The early stages of adulthood are often characterized by long hours spent building a career, establishing a professional reputation, and working towards goals that may take years to achieve. It's easy to become consumed by work, especially when ambition and the desire for success drive her forward.

At the same time, maintaining personal relationships, self-care, and mental well-being is just as important. Learning how to set boundaries between work and personal life is a critical responsibility during this period. Overworking can lead to burnout, while neglecting personal relationships can leave a young woman feeling isolated. It's significant to develop a routine that allows for both professional growth and personal fulfillment.

Consider the example of someone working long hours in a demanding job, perhaps in an industry that requires dedication and focus. Without the ability to set boundaries, this young woman might find herself sacrificing weekends, missing out on social events, or losing touch with hobbies she once enjoyed. Over time, this lack of balance can lead to burnout or a sense of dissatisfaction, even if she's excelling in her career.

Learning to say no and establish boundaries is a key part of taking responsibility for her well-being. Whether that means setting specific work hours, prioritizing downtime, or making time for loved ones, finding balance helps to ensure that she remains both productive and personally fulfilled.

Personal Accountability and Decision-Making:

As responsibilities increase, personal accountability becomes a central theme. A young woman must learn to take ownership of her decisions and actions. This means accepting both the successes and failures that come with independence. Whether it's a financial mistake, a career misstep, or a conflict in a relationship, she must learn to navigate these challenges with maturity and grace.

Personal accountability also involves recognizing when help is needed. The responsibility of independence doesn't mean going it alone. Learning when to ask for advice or seek support from mentors, friends, or family members is a crucial aspect of adulthood. It's important to acknowledge that no one has all the answers and that asking for help is not a sign of weakness but of wisdom.

Each decision a young woman makes, whether it's choosing a career path, ending or beginning a relationship, or deciding where to live, helps shape her future. The weight of these decisions can feel heavy at times, but they also offer her the chance to take control of her life and chart her own course. Although mistakes are unavoidable, they also present chances for development. Learning to view setbacks as learning experiences rather than failures is a critical mindset that will serve her well throughout life.

The Emotional Weight of Responsibility:

With increased responsibility comes the emotional weight of adulthood. The excitement of independence can sometimes be overshadowed by feelings of stress, anxiety, or even loneliness. Many young women struggle with the pressure to "have it all together" and may feel overwhelmed by the sheer number of responsibilities they are juggling. This emotional weight can lead to self-doubt, making it hard to stay motivated or focused.

It's important for a young woman to recognize that she doesn't have to be perfect. Managing multiple responsibilities is difficult for everyone, and it's okay to feel overwhelmed at times. Building emotional resilience is just as indispensable as managing financial or professional responsibilities. Developing healthy coping mechanisms, such as practicing mindfulness, engaging in regular physical activity, or maintaining a strong support network, can help alleviate some of the emotional burdens that come with this phase of life.

Practical Takeaways:

1. Create a Budget: Start by tracking all your expenses for a month to understand your spending habits. Then, create a budget that prioritizes essential expenses, savings, and personal goals.
2. Establish Boundaries: Acknowledge when to say no. Set clear boundaries between work and personal time to maintain balance and avoid burnout.
3. Seek Guidance: Don't hesitate to ask for advice or seek mentorship from trusted individuals. Having someone to provide perspective can be invaluable.
4. Practice Self-Care: Managing responsibilities is essential, but so is taking care of your mental and emotional health. Make time for relaxation, hobbies, and social connections.
5. Embrace Mistakes: Understand that you will make mistakes, and that's okay. Use them as learning opportunities and allow yourself the space to grow from them.

Chapter 4: The Mature Adult - The Mountains of Achievement

As the arid expanse of young adulthood fades into the distance, the journey of women ascends towards a towering horizon, the majestic mountains of mature achievement. This breathtaking terrain, carved by the relentless forces of experience and determination, represents a pivotal phase in the unfolding saga of self-actualization, a crucible where the hard-won lessons of independence and responsibility are put to the ultimate test.

Within this rarefied domain, the mature woman embarks on a quest to conquer the lofty peaks of personal and professional fulfillment, each summit a testament to her unwavering resilience, her hard-earned wisdom, and her indomitable spirit. From the sheer cliffs of career aspirations to the treacherous ridges of work-life balance, every aspect of this rugged landscape demands a combination of skill, perseverance, and an unshakable commitment to reaching ever-greater heights.

Yet, the journey towards these soaring pinnacles is not a solitary endeavor. Just as the mountaineer seeks the guidance of seasoned guides and the camaraderie of fellow climbers, the mature woman must forge alliances and nurture the supportive networks that will sustain her through the challenges that lie ahead. For it is in the shared struggles and triumphs of this arduous ascent that the true bonds of sisterhood are forged, imbuing each woman with the strength and solidarity necessary to conquer even the most formidable obstacles.

As she ascends these towering peaks, the mature woman bears witness to breathtaking vistas of personal growth and self-discovery, each summit offering a panoramic view of the winding path that has led her to this exhilarating vantage point. From these lofty heights, she can survey the landscapes of her past, acknowledging the triumphs and setbacks that have shaped her journey, while also casting her gaze towards the distant horizons that beckon with new challenges and opportunities.

With each arduous step, each precipice navigated, and each summit conquered, the mature woman emerges as a living embodiment of resilience, strength, and hard-won wisdom. The mountains of achievement become not merely a physical terrain, but a metaphorical testament to the indomitable spirit of womanhood, a reminder that with unwavering determination and a steadfast commitment to growth, even the loftiest goals can be attained.

4.1: Climbing Personal and Professional Summits

As a woman progresses into mature adulthood, she faces the challenge of climbing the towering peaks of personal and professional fulfillment. This stage of life is often compared to scaling a mountain, where every step forward requires perseverance, balance, and strategy. The summits she aims for are high and ambitious, but reaching them represents the culmination of her hard work, dreams, and the lessons learned from earlier stages of life. These "mountains" are not only symbolic of career success but also personal growth, relationships, and the ongoing journey of self-actualization.

In this phase, a woman may have already achieved certain milestones, perhaps she has established a career, formed meaningful relationships, or raised a family. Yet, there is a persistent drive to keep climbing, to continue striving for new heights. The peaks of personal and professional success are ever-present, and reaching them requires not only effort but also reflection and intentional choices.

The Pursuit of Professional Success:

One of the most significant aspects of climbing these metaphorical mountains is the pursuit of professional success. For many women, this stage of life is marked by a deep commitment to career growth and the desire to make a meaningful impact in their field. Whether she is striving for leadership roles, building her own business, or contributing to important causes, this pursuit demands dedication and focus.

However, the path to professional success is often fraught with obstacles. Women in the workplace may face gender biases, glass ceilings, and the challenge of balancing career aspirations with other responsibilities. The journey to the top can feel isolating at times, especially in male-dominated industries or leadership positions where women remain underrepresented. Despite these challenges, many women push forward, determined to achieve their goals and break through the barriers that stand in their way.

Take, for example, Ursula von der Leyen, the first female President of the European Commission. Her journey to the top of European politics was not without its challenges, but her persistence, strategic thinking, and commitment to her values allowed her to overcome obstacles and lead in a position of significant influence. Her story is an inspiration to women seeking to make their mark in their respective fields, illustrating the power of resilience and the importance of pursuing one's vision.

For others, the pursuit of professional success may involve starting a business, taking risks, and carving out their own path. Women entrepreneurs face unique challenges but also opportunities to create something that reflects their passions and talents. The success stories of female entrepreneurs, such as Oprah Winfrey or Sara Blakely (founder of Spanx), demonstrate that innovation, determination, and strategic risk-taking can lead to extraordinary achievements.

Yet, the climb toward professional success is not just about reaching a specific job title or income level. It's about the fulfillment that comes from doing meaningful work, contributing to society, and achieving personal goals. For many women, professional success is tied to a sense of purpose, the feeling that their work is making a difference in the lives of others, whether through business, public service, the arts, or education. This sense of purpose is what sustains them through the challenges and setbacks that inevitably arise.

Balancing Personal Fulfillment:

While professional success is an important goal, the climb toward fulfillment also involves achieving balance in personal life. At this stage, many women are juggling multiple roles, partner, parent, professional, community leader, and the demands on their time and energy can feel overwhelming. Learning to balance these roles without losing sight of personal fulfillment is one of the most significant challenges during this phase of life.

This is the point at which work-life balance becomes relevant. Finding equilibrium between the demands of a career and the desire for a rich personal life is critical. Without balance, the pursuit of professional success can lead to burnout, strained relationships, and a sense of dissatisfaction. On the other hand, women who find ways to integrate their personal passions with their professional responsibilities often report greater levels of happiness and fulfillment.

Consider the story of Michelle Obama, who balanced her role as First Lady of the United States with her responsibilities as a mother, wife, and advocate for key social causes. Throughout her time in the White House, she made a conscious effort to maintain balance, ensuring that her family remained a priority while also pursuing initiatives related to education, health, and military families. Her ability to juggle these roles with grace and authenticity is a model for women striving to achieve both personal and professional fulfillment.

Achieving this balance requires setting boundaries, learning to delegate, and being intentional about how time and energy are spent. It also involves prioritizing self-care, a concept that is frequently overlooked in the pursuit of success. Taking time for relaxation, hobbies, and relationships is not a luxury but a necessity for maintaining emotional and physical well-being. The ability to care for oneself, while also meeting the demands of career and family, is a key factor in long-term success.

The Role of Resilience:

As a woman climbs toward her personal and professional summits, resilience becomes one of her most valuable assets. The journey is rarely smooth; there will be setbacks, failures, and moments of doubt. The ability to recover from these challenges, to learn from them, and to continue moving forward is what separates those who reach the top from those who give up along the way.

Resilience is built over time, often through the very difficulties that seem insurmountable at the moment. Women who have faced adversity, whether personal, financial, or professional, typically emerge stronger and more determined. Take the example of Viola Davis, who overcame significant challenges in her early life to become one of the most celebrated actresses of her generation. Her story is a testament to the power of resilience, demonstrating that setbacks are not the end of the road but an opportunity for growth.

The climb toward success also requires the ability to adapt. As a woman moves through different stages of life, her priorities may shift, and the goals she once pursued may no longer hold the same importance. Adapting to these changes, while staying true to her values, allows her to continue growing and evolving, even as the landscape of her life changes.

Practical Takeaways:

1. Define Success for Yourself: Success means different things to different people. Take time to reflect on what success looks like for you, both personally and professionally. Make sure your goals align with your values and passions.
2. Set Boundaries: To achieve balance, set clear boundaries between work and personal life. Protect your time for self-care and relationships, and avoid the temptation to overextend yourself.

3. Develop Resilience: See failures as chances for improvement. Learn from failures, and use them to build the resilience needed to continue pursuing your goals.
4. Seek Support Networks: Surround yourself with mentors, colleagues, and friends who can provide encouragement, advice, and perspective. Having a strong support network can make the climb toward success less isolating and more fulfilling.
5. Adapt to Change: Recognize that your goals and priorities may shift over time. Be flexible and open to new opportunities, even if they take you in a different direction than you originally planned.

4.2: Managing Multiple Roles

As a woman ascends the mountains of success in mature adulthood, she often finds herself balancing multiple, sometimes conflicting, roles. This stage of life is marked by a convergence of responsibilities: career, family, friendships, community, and self-care. Each role requires time, energy, and commitment, and the art of managing these diverse responsibilities becomes essential. Balancing these roles is a skill developed over time, one that calls for adaptability, resilience, and frequently a keen sense of prioritization. Navigating the demands of multiple roles while pursuing personal and professional growth is akin to climbing a mountain with various peaks, each one representing a different aspect of her life that requires attention, effort, and skill to reach.

The concept of "having it all" regularly looms large in mature adulthood. Society frequently suggests that a successful woman should be able to excel at work, nurture her family, and maintain a fulfilling personal life, all without missing a beat. However, this ideal is not only unrealistic but also unsustainable. Learning to set boundaries, delegate responsibilities, and prioritize self-care becomes crucial to her well-being and long-term success.

The Demands of Career and Professional Growth:

For many women, career and professional growth remain central components of their lives in mature adulthood. By this stage, she may have established herself in her field, advanced to a leadership role, or even started her own business. The pursuit of professional goals requires time and dedication, often with long hours and high expectations. Yet, this commitment to career success doesn't diminish her responsibilities in other areas, and the challenge of balancing a demanding career with personal obligations is a reality many women face.

Workplace expectations can make it difficult to draw boundaries between professional and personal life, especially in competitive fields where "always being available" is valued. This is particularly challenging for women who are also primary caregivers at home. They may feel pressured to prove their dedication to work by putting in extra hours, even if it means sacrificing time with family or for self-care. Finding balance requires a conscious effort to establish boundaries, such as setting specific work hours or learning to say no to additional responsibilities that could compromise her personal life.

Consider the example of Sheryl Sandberg, former COO of Facebook, who has spoken openly about the challenges of balancing a demanding career with family life. Her candid discussions about prioritizing work-life balance and the need to "lean in" without burning out resonate with many women striving to achieve professional success while managing multiple roles. Sandberg's story illustrates that even those who reach the highest levels of career success grapple with the difficulty of balancing work and personal commitments.

The Role of Family and Parenting:

In mature adulthood, many women find themselves juggling family roles, from nurturing children to supporting aging parents or maintaining a strong relationship with a partner. Parenthood, in particular, is a significant commitment, with young children needing constant attention and guidance. Meanwhile, as parents age, daughters often step into a caregiving role, adding another layer of responsibility to their lives.

These family roles can be incredibly rewarding, but they also demand time, energy, and emotional investment. A woman may feel the pull to be a present and supportive mother, partner, or caregiver, which can make balancing career ambitions and personal needs all the more challenging. The stress of managing these responsibilities can sometimes lead to feelings of guilt, especially if she feels she is falling short in one area while focusing on another.

Parenthood itself requires flexibility and adaptability, as each stage of a child's life presents new challenges. For a woman with young children, the demands may include managing school schedules, attending extracurricular activities, and handling daily household tasks. For those with teenage children, the role may shift toward providing emotional support and guidance. Each stage brings unique demands that can affect her ability to focus on other areas of her life.

Maintaining Personal Health and Self-Care:

Amid the demands of career, family, and social roles, personal health and self-care are often neglected. However, maintaining physical, mental, and emotional well-being is essential for effectively managing multiple responsibilities. The importance of self-care cannot be overstated, as it allows a woman to recharge, reduce stress, and stay resilient in the face of challenges. Neglecting self-care, on the other hand, can lead to burnout, fatigue, and even physical health issues that may prevent her from fully engaging in her roles.

For many women, finding time for self-care feels indulgent, especially when there are so many pressing demands on their time. However, reframing self-care as a necessity rather than a luxury can help overcome this hesitation. Simple practices, such as regular exercise, meditation, and setting aside time for hobbies, contribute significantly to mental clarity and emotional stability. A woman who prioritizes self-care is better equipped to manage stress and remain effective in her various roles.

Mindfulness practices can also be beneficial, helping her remain present and focused amid her many responsibilities. Research suggests that mindfulness not only reduces stress but also improves decision-making and emotional regulation, skills that are invaluable for someone managing multiple roles. By taking care of her own needs, she becomes more resilient, enabling her to give more fully to her family, work, and community.

Building a Support Network:

Managing multiple roles is not a solo endeavor, and building a strong support network is essential. For many women, support comes from a variety of sources: family, friends, colleagues, mentors, and community members. Asking for help and delegating tasks are vital skills for maintaining balance and avoiding burnout. Whether it's sharing household responsibilities with a partner, enlisting the help of family members in caregiving, or collaborating with colleagues on work projects, delegating can lighten the load and provide a sense of shared responsibility.

In the workplace, professional support networks can offer both emotional support and practical advice on managing career and personal demands. A mentor or peer who understands the pressures of balancing work with family life can provide insights, encouragement, and sometimes even opportunities for flexibility. Women who cultivate these connections often find that they are better able to manage the demands of their multiple roles.

Similarly, community connections, such as neighborhood groups, parent organizations, or support groups, can offer additional resources and camaraderie. Being part of a supportive community creates a sense of shared experience, helping to alleviate the feeling of isolation that sometimes accompanies the pressures of mature adulthood.

Practical Takeaways:

1. Set Boundaries: Clearly define boundaries between work, family, and personal time. Hold yourself accountable to these boundaries and let others know about them.
2. Make Self-Care a Priority: Make self-care an essential component of your daily schedule. Regular exercise, adequate rest, and hobbies that bring joy contribute to resilience and well-being.
3. Delegate Responsibilities: Don't be afraid to ask for help. Share household and family responsibilities with partners, family members, or friends, and delegate tasks at work when possible.
4. Seek Support Networks: Build a network of supportive friends, colleagues, and mentors who understand your challenges. Surrounding yourself with people who can offer advice, perspective, and assistance makes managing multiple roles more feasible.
5. Practice Mindfulness: Incorporate mindfulness practices, such as meditation or deep breathing exercises, into your daily routine to reduce stress and enhance focus.

Chapter 5: Intersectionality - The Crossroads of Identity

Throughout the winding journey that is the geography of women, a constant thread emerges, the intricate interplay of diverse identities that shape and mold the lived experiences of every individual. This intersection of race, ethnicity, socioeconomic status, sexual orientation, and myriad other facets of selfhood creates a rich tapestry, a multi-hued canvas upon which the narratives of women are woven.

At the crossroads of these intersecting identities lies a landscape of both challenge and opportunity. The struggles born of systemic inequities and societal biases coexist with the profound beauty and resilience that emerges from the embrace of one's authentic self.

Within this intricate weave, the journey of self-discovery and self-actualization takes on heightened significance, as each woman must navigate the unique obstacles and triumphs that arise from her distinct positionality. The path that one individual treads may be paved with barriers and roadblocks, while another's route is illuminated by the privileges and advantages bestowed by societal constructs.

Yet, regardless of the terrain, the call to embrace the multidimensional nature of women echoes across all landscapes. For it is in the celebration of our diverse identities, in the acknowledgment of our shared struggles and triumphs, that we find the strength and solidarity to forge ahead. We are united in our pursuit of equity, empowerment, and a more just and inclusive world.

As we traverse this intricate crossroads, we bear witness to the resilience and tenacity of those who have paved the way before us, their footsteps etched into the very fabric of our collective journey. Their stories, their sacrifices, and their unwavering determination serve as beacons, guiding us towards a future where the tapestry of women is not merely acknowledged but celebrated in all its vibrant, multifaceted splendor.

It is within the intricate weave of intersectionality that we find the true essence of women – a tapestry woven from the threads of resilience, courage, and an unwavering commitment to embracing the richness of our diverse identities. For it is in the harmonious coexistence of our differences that we discover the beauty and strength that lies at the heart of our shared humanity.

5.1 The Intersection of Gender, Race, Culture, and Class

In today's complex world, a woman's identity is shaped by an intricate blend of gender, race, culture, and class, which intersect to form her unique experiences, challenges, and perspectives. This concept of intersectionality, first introduced by legal scholar Kimberlé Crenshaw, recognizes that identities are not isolated or separate but rather interwoven to create multidimensional experiences that influence a woman's life in profound ways. Intersectionality helps us see how the convergence of gender with race, culture, and socioeconomic background amplifies both privilege and discrimination, resulting in unique struggles and strengths. Understanding these intersections allows for a more nuanced appreciation of a woman's journey, honoring her resilience and the diversity of her identity.

Each facet of a woman's identity, whether it be her race, cultural background, or economic status, adds depth and complexity to her life. A woman of color from a low-income background, for example, may face a different set of societal expectations, barriers, and opportunities than a white woman from an affluent family. These intersecting factors influence her worldview, relationships, career choices, and sense of self. Recognizing and appreciating the significance of intersectionality is key to supporting women from diverse backgrounds and creating inclusive spaces that respect all aspects of their identity.

Gender and Race: Navigating Dual Layers of Bias

The intersection of gender and race creates unique challenges for women of color, who often face both gender-based and racial discrimination. These women navigate a world in which societal biases related to both their gender and race frequently intersect, resulting in unique experiences of marginalization and resilience. A Black woman in the workplace, for instance, may face stereotypes that question her authority or competency in ways that white women or men of color might not. This dual discrimination creates obstacles in her career advancement, self-expression, and professional relationships, requiring her to constantly prove her worth.

Moreover, women of color are frequently underrepresented in leadership roles and high-paying industries, partly due to systemic biases and structural inequities. Studies show that Black, Latinx, and Indigenous women earn less than their white counterparts, even with similar education and experience. This pay gap is not only a reflection of gender bias, but also of the racial inequities that affect women of color specifically. Women from marginalized racial backgrounds often find themselves navigating environments that fail to recognize their contributions, limiting their opportunities for professional growth.

Yet, women of color demonstrate remarkable resilience and strength in the face of these challenges. Take, for example, the legacy of Rosa Parks, who became a symbol of courage and defiance in the Civil Rights Movement. Her actions demonstrated not only the resilience of Black women, but also their critical role in advocating for social change. Rosa Parks's intersectional identity as a Black woman allowed her to highlight both racial and gender injustices, creating a lasting impact on future generations and inspiring women of color to stand up for their rights.

Cultural Identity: The Influence of Heritage and Tradition

A woman's cultural background plays an essential role in shaping her worldview, values, and sense of self. Cultural traditions, practices, and expectations can be both sources of strength and points of tension as she navigates her identity. For many women, culture is a cherished part of their identity, providing a sense of belonging, continuity, and purpose. However, cultural expectations can sometimes create pressure, especially if they conflict with her personal goals or values.

For instance, a woman from a traditional background may face expectations related to marriage, family roles, or career choices that differ from her own aspirations. These cultural norms can sometimes feel restrictive, as she balances the desire to honor her heritage with her individual dreams. A woman of South Asian descent, for example, might feel societal pressure to prioritize marriage over career ambitions, leading to an internal conflict between her cultural values and her personal aspirations.

Yet, many women find ways to reconcile these aspects, blending cultural heritage with individual expression. Malala Yousafzai, the Pakistani activist and Nobel Laureate, exemplifies how cultural identity can be both a challenge and a source of inspiration. Growing up in a culture that discouraged girls' education, Malala not only defied these expectations but also advocated for change within her community. Her intersectional identity as a Muslim woman from Pakistan allowed her to raise awareness about the importance of education for girls worldwide, highlighting the transformative power of cultural pride combined with the courage to challenge limiting norms.

Class and Economic Status: Navigating Socioeconomic Barriers

Economic status adds another dimension to a woman's experience, affecting her access to education, healthcare, and career opportunities. Women from lower-income backgrounds face unique challenges, including limited financial resources, reduced access to quality education, and fewer professional networks. These barriers can hinder her ability to pursue her ambitions, making the journey toward financial independence and professional success more difficult. Socioeconomic challenges often intersect with racial and gender biases, further limiting opportunities for women from marginalized backgrounds.

For example, a Latina woman from a low-income neighborhood may encounter numerous systemic obstacles in accessing higher education or entering certain career fields. These barriers not only limit her career prospects but also reinforce societal inequalities, as she must work harder to achieve the same level of success as someone from a more privileged background. Socioeconomic inequities also impact mental and physical health, as low-income women frequently have limited access to healthcare and wellness resources, impacting their overall well-being.

Despite these challenges, many women from low-income backgrounds demonstrate resilience, determination, and innovation. The story of Dolores Huerta, a labor leader and civil rights activist who co-founded the United Farm Workers, illustrates how economic disadvantage can inspire a commitment to social change. Huerta's advocacy for labor rights emerged from her understanding of the struggles faced by low-income farmworkers, many of whom were women. Her intersectional identity as a Latina and a labor advocate allowed her to address issues of both economic justice and gender equality, making a lasting impact on labor rights in the U.S.

The Power of Intersectional Solidarity

Understanding the intersection of gender, race, culture, and class highlights the importance of solidarity across diverse identities. When women come together with an awareness of their unique and shared experiences, they can advocate for broader social changes that benefit everyone. Building inclusive communities that honor the diverse identities of all women fosters empathy, strengthens connections, and creates an environment in which each woman's story is valued.

This intersectional solidarity is particularly important in advocating for policy changes that address issues like equal pay, healthcare access, and educational opportunities for all women. For instance, policies that support affordable childcare, equal pay, and anti-discrimination measures benefit women across different backgrounds, especially those who face multiple layers of marginalization. By standing together, women can amplify each other's voices, advocate for inclusive policies, and work toward a society that respects and values all identities.

Practical Takeaways:

1. Acknowledge Intersectionality: Reflect on the intersecting aspects of your identity, such as race, culture, and class, that shape your experiences. Recognize and appreciate how these layers contribute to your unique strengths and perspectives.

2. Advocate for Inclusivity: Support initiatives and organizations that promote diversity and inclusion, both within and outside the workplace. Encourage conversations and actions that honor intersectional identities.

3. Foster Solidarity: Build connections with women from different backgrounds, creating an inclusive community that celebrates diversity. Learn from others' experiences and offer support and understanding.

4. Support Intersectional Policies: Advocate for policies that address intersectional issues, such as fair wages, healthcare access, and anti-discrimination measures, which benefit women across diverse backgrounds.

5. Honor Cultural Heritage: Embrace and celebrate your cultural background, finding ways to blend your heritage with your personal values and goals, creating a unique and fulfilling identity.

5.2: Navigating Diverse Landscapes of Experience

For women, the journey of self-discovery and fulfillment is shaped by a constellation of social, cultural, and personal factors that intersect to create unique, multifaceted experiences. The concept of intersectionality, introduced by Kimberlé Crenshaw, offers a framework for understanding how overlapping identities, such as race, class, culture, sexuality, and disability, interact to shape individual experiences. For women, navigating these diverse landscapes means grappling with both the universal aspects of womanhood and the distinct challenges and strengths that arise from their unique combinations of identity. This intersectional approach helps us appreciate the rich diversity of women's experiences and fosters empathy and solidarity across different backgrounds.

Intersectionality acknowledges that no two women experience the world in exactly the same way. A woman's life is influenced not only by her gender but also by the racial, socioeconomic, cultural, and other identities she carries. These intersecting factors create a mosaic of lived experiences that shape her worldview, opportunities, and challenges. By understanding intersectionality, women, and those around them, gain insight into the nuanced ways their identities affect their lives, informing how they approach their personal, professional, and social spheres.

Cultural Heritage and Identity:

A woman's cultural heritage plays a crucial role in shaping her identity and guiding her values. Cultural backgrounds often provide a sense of connection, pride, and tradition, serving as a foundation for self-expression and purpose. For many women, family traditions and cultural expectations create a framework within which they navigate life's decisions and relationships. However, these cultural norms can also create internal conflict, especially when personal aspirations clash with traditional expectations.

Imagine a young woman from a conservative family who is encouraged to prioritize family and marriage over career ambitions. While she may feel a deep respect for her cultural heritage, she may also struggle with the desire to pursue her own professional goals. Balancing these cultural expectations with personal dreams can be challenging, especially if her choices diverge from family or societal norms. The process of negotiating her own path, while honoring her heritage, is both enriching and complex.

An example of this balance can be seen in the life of Malala Yousafzai, the Pakistani activist for girls' education. Growing up in a region where girls' education was discouraged, Malala navigated the intersection of her cultural identity and her commitment to equal rights. Her journey illustrates how women can challenge cultural limitations while respecting their heritage, contributing to broader social change. Malala's story demonstrates the strength required to advocate for personal values within traditional frameworks, highlighting how intersectionality shapes the pursuit of self-expression and identity.

Navigating Racial and Ethnic Identity:

For women of color, race, and ethnicity add another layer to the experience of women. Racism and prejudice remain pervasive in many societies, influencing access to education, employment, healthcare, and representation in media and politics. These experiences create a dual challenge for women of color, who often face both gender-based and racial discrimination. Navigating these intersecting identities requires resilience and self-awareness, as women of color learn to reconcile their sense of self with societal expectations and stereotypes.

Career challenges illustrate the impact of these intersecting identities. Women of color are regularly underrepresented in leadership roles and face higher hurdles in advancing within their fields, not only because of gender but also due to racial biases. Studies show that Black, Indigenous, and Latinx women frequently earn less than their white counterparts and encounter unique forms of microaggressions in professional settings. The pressure to conform to dominant cultural norms can lead to feelings of isolation or inadequacy.

A prominent example of overcoming these obstacles is the story of Maya Angelou. Growing up in the racially segregated South, Angelou faced the harsh realities of racial discrimination. Despite these barriers, she emerged as a powerful voice in literature, civil rights, and women's rights, using her work to challenge racial and gender stereotypes. Angelou's resilience and dedication to her craft highlight the strength that many women of color bring to their communities, even as they confront adversity.

The Impact of Socioeconomic Background:

Class and socioeconomic status are additional factors that intersect with gender to shape women's experiences. Women from low-income backgrounds often face limited access to quality education, healthcare, and career opportunities. Financial insecurity can add stress to a woman's life, affecting her mental and physical well-being, and limiting her ability to pursue personal and professional goals.

Socioeconomic challenges are typically compounded by other forms of discrimination. A woman who is both low-income and a member of a minority group may face multiple layers of disadvantage, struggling not only with financial hardship but also with societal biases. Despite these barriers, women from all socioeconomic backgrounds demonstrate remarkable resilience, creativity, and resourcefulness in finding ways to improve their circumstances and provide for their families.

Consider the story of Dolores Huerta, a labor leader and civil rights activist who co-founded the United Farm Workers. Born into a working-class family, Huerta dedicated her life to advocating for the rights of migrant farmworkers, many of whom were women facing economic and social oppression. Her advocacy for labor rights and social justice exemplifies the strength that women bring to their communities, especially when their identities intersect with socioeconomic challenges. Huerta's legacy is a reminder of how intersectionality can inspire women to fight for change not only for themselves but also for their communities.

Sexual Orientation and Gender Identity:

Sexual orientation and gender identity add further complexity to a woman's experience, especially in a world where LGBTQIA+ individuals often face discrimination, lack of acceptance, and limited legal protections. For a woman who identifies as LGBTQIA+, navigating both her gender and sexual identity can create unique challenges. Fear of rejection, societal stigma, and sometimes even hostility from family members or peers can make self-acceptance and public expression difficult.

LGBTQIA+ women have made significant contributions to social movements and have been instrumental in advocating for equality. Audre Lorde, a Black lesbian poet and activist, is a powerful example of how LGBTQIA+ women have used their voices to champion intersectional justice. Through her writing and activism, Lorde emphasized the importance of recognizing the diverse experiences of women and the need for solidarity across identities. Her work underscores the idea that the fight for equality and justice must include all women, acknowledging their unique journeys and struggles.

Fostering Solidarity and Inclusivity:

Understanding intersectionality emphasizes the importance of fostering inclusive spaces that honor the diverse experiences of all women. When women from different backgrounds come together, they bring unique perspectives that enrich discussions and inspire comprehensive approaches to addressing inequality. Inclusive communities encourage empathy, allowing women to see the world through the lens of each other's experiences and build bridges across their differences.

This solidarity is vital for creating lasting social change. When women unite, acknowledging both shared struggles and unique challenges, they are better equipped to advocate for policies and initiatives that benefit all women. Inclusive spaces allow women to learn from each other's strengths and resilience, inspiring mutual growth and understanding. Organizations that promote diversity and inclusion, whether in the workplace, schools, or community groups, play a crucial role in fostering this kind of solidarity and ensuring that all voices are valued.

Practical Takeaways:

1. Reflect on Intersectionality: Take time to reflect on the various aspects of your identity, such as race, class, and culture, and how they shape your experiences. Recognize that each person's background offers a unique perspective.
2. Support Diverse Voices: Actively seek to amplify the voices of women from marginalized communities. Creating space for diverse stories fosters empathy, inclusivity, and progress.
3. Build Inclusive Communities: Whether in professional, social, or personal settings, promote inclusivity by encouraging open dialogue and mutual respect. Embrace and celebrate differences to create an environment where everyone feels valued.
4. Educate and Advocate: Continue learning about the unique challenges faced by women with intersecting identities. Advocate for policies and practices that promote equity, inclusion, and social justice, recognizing the importance of intersectionality.

Chapter 6: Maturity - The Forest of Wisdom

As the journey through the geography of women progresses, the rugged terrain of personal and professional achievement gradually gives way to a verdant landscape. The forest of maturity, a verdant sanctuary where the hard-won lessons of life coalesce into a tapestry of wisdom and self-acceptance.

Within this evergreen expanse, the mature woman finds herself surrounded by a canopy of experiences, each branch bearing the fruit of knowledge and growth. The winding paths that have led her to this tranquil refuge are etched into the very bark of the ancient trees, serving as a vivid reminder of the triumphs and challenges that have shaped her evolution.

Yet, this forest is not merely a passive spectator to the unfolding saga of women; rather, it is a living, breathing entity, its roots intertwined with the collective narratives of those who have walked its verdant trails before. The wisdom imparted by mentors, elders, and kindred spirits echoes through the gentle rustling of leaves, offering guidance and solace to those who seek to navigate the complexities of this verdant domain.

As the mature woman ventures deeper into this sylvan sanctuary, she is confronted with the opportunity to shed the burdens of societal expectations and limiting beliefs. She allows her true self to blossom and flourish amidst the nurturing embrace of nature's eternal cycles. It is here, within the dappled light and the symphony of birdsong, that she can embrace the beauty of her authentic identity, free from the constraints that once bound her.

The forest of maturity is not merely a physical landscape, but a metaphorical representation of the journey towards self-acceptance, growth, and inner peace. Its winding paths invite the mature woman to explore the depths of her own psyche, to confront the fears and insecurities that have hindered her progress. She emerges victorious, emboldened by the wisdom and resilience that have been cultivated through a lifetime of experiences.

As she traverses this verdant expanse, the mature woman bears witness to the cycles of renewal and regeneration that permeate every aspect of the natural world. Reminding her of the enduring strength and resilience that lie at the core of women. For in the forest of maturity, the journey towards self-actualization is not a solitary endeavor, but a harmonious dance with the rhythms of life itself.

6.1: Reflecting on the Journey

As a woman enters maturity, she finds herself in the "Forest of Wisdom," a space where the experiences of her life come together to form a cohesive understanding of who she is. Each stage of her journey, from childhood through young adulthood to mature adulthood, has contributed to her growth, resilience, and wisdom. Reflecting on this journey is both a privilege and a powerful act of self-acknowledgment, allowing her to understand how each moment, challenge, and victory has added depth and richness to her identity. The Forest of Wisdom, much like the forest itself, is dense with memories, insights, and lessons learned along the way.

Reflection is more than reminiscing; it is an intentional act of self-discovery and acceptance. By revisiting the different chapters of her life, a woman gains clarity about the values she holds, the growth she has achieved, and the strength she has developed. This reflection allows her to celebrate her accomplishments, make peace with past mistakes, and embrace the wisdom she has cultivated. It is through this process of reflection that she becomes fully aware of the journey she has undertaken, a journey marked by resilience, courage, and the unique beauty of her lived experiences.

Childhood: The Roots of Self-Worth and Belonging

Reflecting on childhood is often like looking back at the roots of a strong tree. The experiences of childhood, family bonds, early friendships, and first accomplishments, serve as the foundation of a woman's self-worth and sense of belonging. These memories are filled with moments of curiosity and innocence, times when life's challenges were simpler and her confidence was shaped by the encouragement and support of those around her.

Revisiting these early years allows her to reconnect with her original sense of wonder, curiosity, and creativity. She may remember the sense of adventure she felt exploring the world for the first time, or the comfort of knowing she was loved and cared for. For women who experienced difficult childhoods, reflection can be a healing process, allowing them to honor the resilience that enabled them to persevere. Recognizing the formative role of childhood helps her appreciate how far she has come and how deeply her foundation has influenced her journey.

Adolescence: The Seeds of Identity and Self-Discovery

Adolescence is a time of self-discovery, where a young woman begins to cultivate her sense of identity and independence. Reflecting on this transformative stage, she recalls the intense emotions, friendships, and first experiences that began to shape her understanding of herself and her place in the world. It is a period often marked by both the desire for acceptance and the search for authenticity.

As she looks back on adolescence, she may recognize the courage it took to navigate peer pressure, identity formation, and the balancing act of conforming while finding her own voice. It was in these moments of conflict and exploration that she learned about resilience, values, and the importance of standing firm in her beliefs. Even if she made choices she now views differently, the wisdom gained from these experiences helped her become the person she is today.

Reflecting on adolescence also allows her to appreciate the friendships and connections that offered support and companionship during this time. These relationships were formative, teaching her about trust, empathy, and the power of companionship. Through reflection, she can acknowledge the importance of these connections, which may have shaped her values and approach to relationships throughout her life.

Young Adulthood: The Pursuit of Dreams and Independence

Young adulthood is a stage filled with ambition, dreams, and the quest for independence. For many women, it is a time marked by significant choices related to career, relationships, and personal goals. Reflecting on this period allows her to revisit the enthusiasm and courage with which she pursued her dreams, took risks, and made decisions that set her on her unique path.

The challenges of young adulthood often center on finding direction and making life-defining choices. In reflecting on this period, a woman may feel a sense of pride for the obstacles she overcame and the courage she showed in forging her path. She might also recognize how her perspective has evolved, seeing the decisions she once agonized over with a newfound sense of acceptance or even humor. Looking back, she may appreciate both the successes and the mistakes, understanding that each decision contributed to her growth and resilience.

This period may also include forming significant relationships, such as marriage or long-term partnerships, and, for some, starting a family. Reflecting on these experiences allows her to honor the sacrifices and commitments she made, celebrating the love, joy, and shared goals that these relationships brought into her life. The challenges faced in balancing personal goals with partnership and family responsibilities taught her invaluable lessons about compromise, empathy, and unconditional love.

Mature Adulthood: Balancing Multiple Roles and Building Resilience

Mature adulthood often brings an intricate balancing act, as a woman manages multiple roles, career, family, community, and self-care. This stage is marked by both external achievements and internal growth, as she builds resilience, adapts to changing demands, and deepens her understanding of herself and others. Reflecting on mature adulthood allows her to acknowledge the strength required to juggle these responsibilities, as well as the growth achieved through these experiences.

In this stage, a woman may have reached certain milestones, career accomplishments, raising children, or contributing to her community. Reflecting on these achievements allows her to appreciate the resilience and dedication she exhibited. She has learned to navigate the complexities of life with grace, balancing her aspirations with the needs of her loved ones. She may also recognize the importance of self-care and boundaries, understanding that tending to her well-being has been essential in sustaining her roles and responsibilities.

This period of life may also bring the realization that success is not solely defined by external achievements, but by the quality of her relationships, her well-being, and her sense of inner peace. This insight, gained through years of experience, allows her to redefine what truly matters and to focus on the aspects of life that bring her fulfillment and joy.

Embracing the Wisdom of the Journey

The Forest of Wisdom is not just a metaphor for reflection; it is a place of celebration, growth, and gratitude. As a woman reflects on her journey, she acknowledges the full spectrum of her experiences, from moments of joy and triumph to times of sorrow and loss. This wisdom, gained through decades of life, empowers her to face the future with confidence and compassion.

Reflecting on the journey also allows her to connect with her purpose. She may feel a renewed sense of commitment to her goals, a desire to share her wisdom with younger generations, or a peaceful acceptance of the life she has lived. Embracing the wisdom of her journey helps her see that each experience, whether joyful or challenging, has contributed to her growth, making her the person she is today.

Practical Takeaways:

1. Celebrate Growth: Recognize the growth achieved at each stage of life. Take pride in both accomplishments and challenges overcome.
2. Embrace Self-Compassion: Reflect on mistakes with compassion, understanding that they contributed to your wisdom and growth.
3. Prioritize Inner Peace: Focus on the aspects of life that bring you fulfillment, relationships, personal passions, and self-care.
4. Share Your Wisdom: Consider sharing your insights with others, especially younger generations, who may benefit from your experiences.
5. Look Forward with Confidence: Use the wisdom gained to approach the future with confidence, knowing that you are resilient, capable, and wise.

6.2: Transmission and Legacy

In the later stages of life, many women find themselves in the "Forest of Wisdom," a space where they reflect not only on their personal journeys but also on what they will leave behind. Transmission and legacy become central themes, as mature women seek to share their insights, values, and experiences with others. This stage is characterized by a desire to give back to future generations, passing on the lessons they've learned and the wisdom they've gained. Whether through mentorship, storytelling, or community engagement, the act of transmission becomes a powerful way to shape the future and leave a meaningful legacy.

Legacy is more than the tangible assets or accomplishments a woman leaves behind; it's the enduring impact of her values, relationships, and contributions. The legacy she creates is woven from the lessons she has learned, the people she has touched, and the positive changes she has inspired in others. Through her words and actions, she has the opportunity to influence others and leave a lasting mark on the world. In the Forest of Wisdom, she becomes both a guardian of her personal story and a guide for those who will follow in her footsteps.

Mentorship: Sharing Experiences and Guiding the Next Generation

One of the most impactful ways a woman transmits her legacy is through mentorship. By sharing her experiences, insights, and challenges, she offers younger individuals a map for navigating their own journeys. Mentorship is a mutually enriching relationship: while the mentee benefits from the mentor's wisdom, the mentor finds fulfillment in guiding others, reflecting on her own journey, and even gaining fresh perspectives.

In a professional setting, mentorship allows a woman to pass on valuable career knowledge and strategies, helping the next generation navigate the challenges of the workplace. She may offer advice on building confidence, overcoming gender barriers, or balancing work with personal life. Beyond technical skills, she teaches resilience, adaptability, and self-advocacy. For example, a woman who has broken through a glass ceiling in her career can inspire younger women by sharing the lessons she learned along the way, equipping them to face their own challenges.

Mentorship can also extend beyond careers, encompassing life skills, values, and personal growth. By sharing stories of resilience, love, and failure, a woman can teach younger individuals about the importance of authenticity, empathy, and self-compassion. These lessons become part of her legacy, living on in the choices, values, and actions of those she has mentored. This transmission of wisdom helps others feel connected, confident, and prepared for their own journey through life.

Family Legacy: Values, Traditions, and Stories

For many women, family is a primary avenue for transmitting their legacy. Through family traditions, values, and storytelling, she instills in her children and grandchildren a sense of identity and belonging. The stories she shares, whether about her own life, her ancestors, or her cultural heritage, become touchstones for future generations, helping them understand where they come from and who they are.

Family legacy often includes the transmission of core values, such as kindness, integrity, and perseverance. A woman may emphasize the importance of compassion, teaching her children to respect and care for others. She might share the value of resilience by telling stories of times when she faced hardship and emerged stronger. These values become woven into the fabric of her family, shaping how future generations approach their own lives.

Traditions play a significant role in family legacy as well. Whether it's a holiday celebration, a cooking recipe, or a cherished family ritual, these traditions create continuity and a shared sense of identity. For instance, a woman who passes down a traditional family recipe is sharing more than just food; she is preserving memories, culture, and a sense of connection to the past. Family traditions create a bridge between generations, allowing children and grandchildren to feel rooted in something larger than themselves.

Community Engagement: Building a Legacy of Service and Impact

Beyond family and personal mentorship, many women leave a legacy through their contributions to their communities. Community engagement offers an opportunity to make a positive impact on a larger scale, whether through volunteer work, activism, or local leadership. A woman who has spent her life advocating for social justice, supporting local charities, or mentoring youth in her neighborhood creates a legacy of service that inspires others to give back.

Community legacy is built on the principle of collective growth, contributing to a better, more inclusive world for everyone. Consider the legacy of Dolores Huerta, a labor leader and civil rights activist who co-founded the United Farm Workers. Her commitment to advocating for labor rights has inspired countless individuals to continue the fight for social justice. Her legacy lives on not only in the policies she helped change, but in the generations of activists and community members who carry forward her mission.

For women who engage in community service, the impact of their legacy is seen in the lives they touch and the changes they help bring about. Even small acts, such as volunteering at a local shelter or organizing community events, create a ripple effect that influences others to step up and give back. The legacy of community engagement is one of hope, resilience, and collective action, a reminder that one person's efforts can make a difference.

Storytelling and Writing: Capturing Wisdom for Future Generations

For many women, storytelling and writing are powerful tools for preserving and sharing their legacy. Through memoirs, journals, and storytelling, she captures her experiences, reflections, and lessons in a way that can be passed down to future generations. Storytelling allows her to impart wisdom in a personal, accessible format, inviting others to learn from her life journey.

A woman who records her stories in a journal or writes a memoir leaves behind a treasure trove of insights. Her words serve as a guide, helping others understand the values she held dear, the struggles she overcame, and the joys she celebrated. These stories become a part of her legacy, allowing her voice to live on long after she is gone. Storytelling is particularly impactful because it combines personal history with universal lessons, making her wisdom relevant and inspiring for generations to come.

In addition to writing, oral storytelling, whether shared around a family table or in a community setting, allows women to communicate values, culture, and resilience. Storytelling is an ancient art that connects people across time and space, reminding younger generations of their heritage and the strength within them. Through stories, a woman's legacy becomes a living entity, continuing to influence and inspire.

Practical Takeaways:

1. Mentor with Purpose: Embrace mentorship opportunities and share your experiences with younger individuals. Offer guidance, encouragement, and insights that empower them on their journey.
2. Preserve Family Traditions: Pass down family traditions and values. Celebrate and share the cultural practices, stories, and recipes that connect generations.
3. Engage in Community Service: Find ways to contribute to your community. Engage in causes that resonate with you and inspire others to do the same.
4. Record Your Story: Consider journaling or writing a memoir. Capture your life's lessons, values, and experiences in a way that can be shared with future generations.
5. Inspire Through Example: Live your values daily. Demonstrate integrity, kindness, and resilience, allowing your actions to leave a lasting impact on those around you.

Chapter 7: Old Age - The Ocean of Serenity

As the journey through the geography of women reaches its final chapter, the mature woman finds herself standing upon the shores of a vast and breathtaking expanse – the ocean of serenity. A realm where the ebb and flow of life's tides have given way to a profound sense of inner peace and acceptance.

This aquatic domain, with its vast horizons and ever-changing hues, beckons the woman to embark on a journey of self-discovery and contentment. A journey that promises to unveil the depths of wisdom and tranquility that can only be attained through a lifetime of experience and growth.

The gentle lapping of waves upon the shore serves as a soothing melody, a symphony that invites the woman to shed the burdens of her past and embrace the present moment with open arms. For it is in this realm of serenity that she can truly appreciate the rich tapestry of her life's journey, each thread woven with the vibrant hues of triumph, resilience, and hard-won wisdom.

As she gazes out across the vast expanse, she is reminded of the cycles of life that have brought her to this moment. The ebb and flow of joys and sorrows, triumphs and setbacks, all indelibly etched into the very fabric of her being. Yet, within the embrace of the ocean's tranquility, these experiences take on a new hue, a deeper significance that resonates with the wisdom and perspective that can only be cultivated through the passage of time.

The ocean of serenity is not merely a physical realm, but a metaphorical representation of the inner peace and acceptance that blossoms in the twilight years of a woman's life. It is a sanctuary where the tumultuous storms of youth and the rugged terrain of adulthood give way to a profound sense of contentment and self-actualization.

Within this aquatic expanse, the woman finds herself surrounded by a symphony of stories, each wave carrying the echoes of those who have navigated these waters before her. The lessons and insights imparted by mentors, elders, and kindred spirits resonate across the vast expanse, offering guidance and solace to those who seek to embrace the serenity of their final chapter.

As the woman embarks on this tranquil voyage, she is invited to let go of the tethers that once bound her, to embrace the freedom and authenticity that comes with a life well-lived. For it is in the depths of this ocean that she can truly appreciate the beauty and resilience of the human spirit. It is in the act of surrendering to its embrace that she can find the ultimate fulfillment and contentment that lies at the heart of the woman's journey.

7.1: Acceptance of the Passing of Time

As a woman enters the later stages of life, she finds herself by the shores of the "Ocean of Serenity," a place of reflection, wisdom, and acceptance. The metaphor of the ocean evokes a sense of calm, depth, and expansiveness, qualities that come to define this phase. Here, she has the chance to embrace the passing of time, to come to peace with life's inevitable changes, and to appreciate the beauty of her journey. Acceptance of time's flow is a central theme in this stage, allowing her to find tranquility in life's transitions and to cultivate gratitude for all she has experienced.

The passing of time is an unavoidable part of life, yet accepting it fully can be challenging. As she reflects on the decades she has lived, the joys and sorrows she has experienced, and the relationships she has nurtured, a woman in this stage may feel a mix of nostalgia, contentment, and even grief. However, the acceptance of time's passage is not about resignation; it is about recognizing that each moment has contributed to her growth and embracing the peace that comes from this awareness. In the Ocean of Serenity, she learns to let go of regrets, embrace impermanence, and find joy in the present.

Embracing Physical Changes and New Realities

One of the most tangible aspects of aging is the experience of physical change. In old age, the body may not be as strong or agile as it once was, and health concerns can become a part of daily life. Accepting these changes can be challenging, as they often serve as reminders of time's passage. However, viewing physical change with acceptance rather than resistance allows her to appreciate her body as a record of her life, a living testament to the years she has spent walking through the world, growing, learning, and transforming.

Aging gracefully is not about denying or resisting these physical changes but rather about honoring the body's journey. Each wrinkle, scar, or gray hair tells a story of resilience and experience. For many women, embracing these physical markers of time becomes a powerful act of self-acceptance. Instead of mourning the loss of youthful beauty, they find beauty in the wisdom and strength that their bodies represent. In this way, the acceptance of physical changes becomes a form of gratitude for the vessel that has carried them through life.

Many women also find that acceptance of physical limitations brings a newfound appreciation for simplicity and presence. Activities may slow down, but this slowness opens the door to mindful living. She may take greater pleasure in simple joys, like walking through a garden, savoring a cup of tea, or sharing a conversation with loved ones. This slowing down is not a loss but a transformation, inviting her to experience life with a deeper sense of awareness and contentment.

Releasing Regrets and Finding Peace

Reflecting on a lifetime inevitably brings memories of choices and actions that, in hindsight, could have been different. Some women carry regrets, missed opportunities, relationships that didn't last, or paths not taken. However, as she stands by the Ocean of Serenity, she has the opportunity to release these regrets and find peace. This release is an act of forgiveness, both for herself and others, allowing her to let go of the past and embrace the present.

Releasing regrets is not about forgetting or minimizing past experiences; it is about accepting them as essential parts of her journey. Each choice, whether perceived as a mistake or a success, contributed to her growth and shaped her understanding of herself and the world. The acceptance of regret is a form of wisdom, recognizing that every decision was made with the knowledge and circumstances of the time. In forgiving herself, she embraces compassion and let's go of the need for perfection.

For many women, this stage also brings a sense of gratitude for the life they have lived, even with its imperfections. Reflecting on the moments of joy, love, resilience, and discovery allows her to see her life as a rich and meaningful story. This perspective helps her find peace, understanding that a life well-lived is not one without challenges or mistakes, but one filled with depth, learning, and personal growth.

Strengthening Relationships and Cherishing Connections

In the later stages of life, relationships often take on even greater importance. The passing of time underscores the value of loved ones, as well as the preciousness of shared moments and memories. A woman in this stage frequently experiences a deepening of her relationships, focusing on quality over quantity and cherishing the people who bring joy, comfort, and meaning to her life.

Old age offers an opportunity to strengthen these connections and to express gratitude to friends, family, and community members who have been part of her journey. She may reach out to reconnect with loved ones, heal old wounds, or simply share time and stories with those close to her. This emphasis on connection brings a profound sense of fulfillment, as she finds comfort in the bonds that have endured over the years.

For many women, this stage also brings the desire to pass down wisdom, values, and traditions. Sharing stories, life lessons, and family history allows her to leave a legacy, enriching the lives of younger generations and ensuring that her insights live on. These conversations are a form of transmission, allowing her to share the fruits of her life's experiences with those who follow.

Embracing Impermanence and the Present Moment

The acceptance of time's passage ultimately leads to an appreciation of impermanence. A woman in this stage of life understands that nothing is permanent, yet rather than finding this realization unsettling, she learns to embrace it. The understanding of impermanence encourages her to live in the present, savoring each moment and letting go of the need to control the future.

In the Ocean of Serenity, impermanence becomes a source of peace. Rather than clinging to past identities or achievements, she allows herself to simply be, finding joy in the here and now. She may develop practices such as mindfulness, meditation, or reflection, which help her stay grounded in the present. This acceptance of impermanence brings a sense of liberation, freeing her from the constraints of regret and the pressures of future ambitions.

Practical Takeaways:

1. Honor Physical Changes: View physical changes as symbols of a life lived fully. Embrace the beauty and strength these changes represent, and find joy in the simplicity of everyday activities.
2. Release Regrets: Let go of regrets by acknowledging them with compassion. Embrace past choices as part of your journey and forgive yourself, allowing peace to replace self-judgment.
3. Deepen Relationships: Strengthen connections with loved ones by expressing gratitude and cherishing shared moments. Invest in meaningful relationships and share your stories and wisdom with those around you.
4. Practice Presence: Embrace impermanence by focusing on the present moment. Cultivate mindfulness and gratitude, finding peace in simply being.

5. Embrace Acceptance: Find solace in the acceptance of life's inevitable transitions. Allow yourself to experience serenity in knowing that each stage of life has brought growth, understanding, and beauty.

7.2: Contemplation of Life

In old age, standing by the metaphorical "Ocean of Serenity," a woman finds herself at a place of deep introspection, a time to contemplate the meaning and essence of her life. This stage is characterized by a gentle acceptance and understanding of the journey she has undertaken, a journey that has been woven with joys, challenges, love, and resilience. The ocean represents not only the vastness of her experiences, but also the calmness and wisdom that come with having lived a full life. Here, she can reflect on her life's purpose, revisit memories, and seek peace in her accomplishments and lessons learned.

Contemplation is a way to honor the life she has lived, a way to bring coherence to a story marked by highs and lows. Rather than seeking answers to unresolved questions or wishing for a different path, she now finds comfort in simply exploring the tapestry of her experiences. By reflecting on the patterns and connections in her life, she gains insight into the themes that have defined her, the people who have enriched her journey, and the legacy she will leave behind.

Exploring Life's Purpose and Meaning

In this contemplative stage, a woman often reflects on the purpose and meaning of her life. Looking back, she may ponder the goals she pursued, the values she upheld, and the impact she has had on others. She may ask herself profound questions: "What did my life stand for?" "How did I make a difference?" "What have I learned?" Her thoughts enable her to reexamine the decisions she made, the aspirations she realized, and even the routes she selected not to pursue, discovering significance in both action and moderation.

For many women, purpose is found not only in personal achievements, but also in the roles they have played in others' lives. Perhaps she finds meaning in the family she has raised, the friendships she has nurtured, or the contributions she has made to her community. Her sense of purpose is often tied to the impact she has had on others, both directly and indirectly, as a mentor, friend, partner, or caregiver. This sense of purpose, even in quiet moments of reflection, brings a profound sense of satisfaction and completeness.

Contemplating life's purpose is also an opportunity to connect with a broader, often spiritual perspective. Many women find comfort in the belief that their lives are part of a larger tapestry that the struggles and successes they have encountered contribute to a greater whole. Spiritual beliefs or a connection with nature can offer reassurance that her life has been meaningful, regardless of the specific achievements or accolades. This sense of connection to something greater allows her to find peace and fulfillment as she contemplates her life's journey.

Revisiting Memories and Cherishing Moments

In the Ocean of Serenity, memories become vivid, treasured companions. A woman in this stage regularly finds herself returning to her most cherished moments, reliving the laughter of family gatherings, the joy of personal milestones, or the quiet beauty of everyday experiences. Revisiting these memories allows her to experience the richness of her life anew, bringing a sense of continuity and fulfillment.

However, this stage is not only about celebrating happy memories; it is also a time to acknowledge and embrace the challenging moments. Reflecting on periods of hardship, loss, or sacrifice reveals her resilience and growth. These experiences, while difficult, have contributed to her character, her strength, and her empathy. She may find that some of her greatest lessons were learned in these moments, and by revisiting them with a compassionate perspective, she comes to see the wisdom she has gained through hardship.

Contemplation of life also includes the memories of people who have passed, whose presence still lives within her. Reflecting on relationships with loved ones who are no longer here can be bittersweet, yet it also brings comfort, as she feels the lasting impact they had on her life. The memories of those who shaped her journey, family members, mentors, friends, become part of her legacy, reminding her of the interconnectedness of human experiences and the continuity of love beyond time.

Accepting Life's Imperfections

In her contemplation, a woman in old age comes to terms with life's imperfections. Reflecting on her choices, she may find moments she wishes had turned out differently. However, in the Ocean of Serenity, acceptance replaces regret. She realizes that life's imperfections and unexpected twists have contributed to her unique path, adding depth and dimension to her story. Contemplating these aspects of her life with compassion, she sees that every experience, whether joyful or painful, contributed to her growth.

Acceptance of imperfection also means recognizing that life's beauty lies in its unpredictability. By allowing herself to let go of the need for control or perfection, she can embrace her journey fully. This acceptance brings a profound sense of peace, as she understands that each moment of her life has unfolded exactly as it was meant to. She finds comfort in knowing that a life well-lived is not flawless but filled with lessons, resilience, and discovery.

Finding Serenity in the Present

The Ocean of Serenity represents not only reflection on the past but also an embrace of the present. In contemplating her life, a woman in this stage finds joy in simple, mindful experiences. The rush of earlier years has slowed, allowing her to savor each moment with a newfound awareness. She may find peace in the natural world, listening to the rustling of leaves, feeling the warmth of the sun, or observing the waves of the ocean. This presence brings a profound sense of contentment, as she realizes that true fulfillment lies in the ability to be fully present.

Many women in this stage turn to practices that nurture their sense of inner peace, such as meditation, mindfulness, or prayer. These practices help her stay grounded, enabling her to appreciate each moment without the distractions of the past or future. This connection to the present brings a sense of unity with the world around her, enhancing her sense of serenity and gratitude.

Preparing for Legacy and Closure

As she contemplates her life, a woman in this stage may also consider her legacy. What values, stories, or wisdom does she wish to pass on? For many, the act of reflection is also an act of transmission, a way to gather the essence of her experiences and share it with loved ones. Preparing for legacy allows her to feel that her life's journey will continue to inspire and guide others, giving her a sense of closure and fulfillment.

She may share stories with family, write letters, or create memories that will live on in the hearts of those she loves. In doing so, she leaves behind not only her story but also her spirit, reminding others of the beauty and strength within each stage of life. Contemplation, in this way, becomes an act of giving, as she offers her insights to those who will continue their own journeys.

Practical Takeaways:

1. Reflect on Purpose: Take time to contemplate the purpose of your life, finding meaning in your contributions and relationships.
2. Cherish Memories: Revisit cherished memories with gratitude, allowing them to bring joy and continuity to your life.
3. Embrace Imperfections: Accept the imperfections in your journey, understanding that they have contributed to your unique path.

4. Practice Presence: Cultivate mindfulness and appreciate the beauty of each moment, embracing the peace that comes from being fully present.
5. Prepare Your Legacy: Consider the wisdom and stories you wish to share. Pass down your insights, values, and love, creating a lasting impact for future generations.

Conclusion

As the ink dries on the final pages of this odyssey through the geography of women, one cannot help but be struck by the sheer depth and richness of the tapestry that has been woven. From the boundless horizons of youth to the verdant sanctuary of maturity, and finally, the tranquil embrace of the ocean of serenity, the journey has been one of profound growth, transformation, and self-discovery.

Throughout these pages, we have borne witness to the innate strength and resilience that lies at the very heart of the feminine spirit. We have seen how women have navigated the rugged terrain of personal and professional challenges, scaling the peaks of triumph and traversing the valleys of adversity with an unwavering determination that is both awe-inspiring and humbling.

Yet, this odyssey has not merely been a celebration of individual accomplishments; rather, it has been a testament to the profound interconnectedness that binds the threads of women together. We have explored the intricate tapestry of mentorship, legacy, and the transmission of wisdom, recognizing that each woman's journey is intricately woven into the greater fabric of human experience.

As we turn the final page, we are left with a renewed sense of appreciation for the beauty and complexity of the feminine experience. We are reminded that womanhood is not a linear path, but rather a rich tapestry of seasons, each one offering its own unique gifts and challenges.

In the end, perhaps the greatest lesson we can take from this odyssey is the power of embracing the present moment, of finding serenity and contentment in the ebb and flow of life's tides. For it is in these moments of deep contemplation and acceptance that we can truly appreciate the depth and significance of the journey itself.

As we close this chapter and embark on new adventures, may we carry with us the wisdom and resilience that have been so beautifully woven into the tapestry of these pages. May we find strength in the knowledge that we are part of a vast and enduring legacy, a tapestry that spans generations and transcends boundaries.

And above all, may we continue to honor and celebrate the infinite beauty and complexity of the feminine spirit. It is in this sacred space that we can truly find the courage and inspiration to navigate the ever-changing landscapes of life with grace, resilience, and an unwavering commitment to growth and self-actualization.

www.ingramcontent.com/pod-product-compliance
Lightning Source LLC
Chambersburg PA
CBHW052224150726

48002CB00003B/1269